A Note From Rick Renner

I am on a personal quest to see a "revival of the Bible" so people can establish their lives on a firm foundation that will stand strong and endure the test when end-time storm winds begin to intensify.

In order to experience a revival of the Bible in your personal life, it is important to take time each day to read, receive, and apply Bible truths to your life. James tells us that if we will continue in the perfect law of liberty — refusing to be forgetful hearers, but determined to be mindful doers — we will be blessed in our ways. As you watch or listen to the programs in this series and work through this corresponding study guide, I trust you will search the Scriptures and allow the Holy Spirit to help you hear something new from God's Word that applies specifically to your life. I encourage you to be a doer of the Word He reveals to you. Whatever the cost, I assure you — it will be worth it.

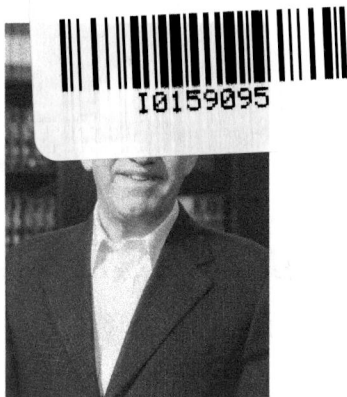

> Thy words were found, and I did eat them;
> and thy word was unto me the joy and rejoicing of mine heart:
> for I am called by thy name, O Lord God of hosts.
> — Jeremiah 15:16

Your brother and friend in Jesus Christ,

Rick Renner

The Infilling of the Holy Spirit

Copyright © 2018 by Rick Renner
8316 E. 73rd St.
Tulsa, Oklahoma 74133

Published by Rick Renner Ministries
www.renner.org

ISBN 13: 978-1-68031-595-0

eBook ISBN 13: 978-1-68031-633-9

How To Use This Study Guide

This five-lesson study guide corresponds to *"The Infilling of the Holy Spirit" With Rick Renner* (Renner TV). Each lesson in this study guide covers a topic that is addressed during the program series, with questions and references supplied to draw you deeper into your own private study of the Scriptures on this subject.

To derive the most benefit from this study guide, consider the following:

First, watch or listen to the program prior to working through the corresponding lesson in this guide. (Programs can also be viewed at **renner.org** by clicking on the Media/Archives links.)

Second, take the time to look up the scriptures included in each lesson. Prayerfully consider their application to your own life.

Third, use a journal or notebook to make note of your answers to each lesson's Study Questions and Practical Application challenges.

Fourth, invest specific time in prayer and in the Word of God to consult with the Holy Spirit. Write down the scriptures or insights He reveals to you about being filled with the Spirit and empowered by Him in your daily life.

Finally, take action! Whatever the Lord tells you to do according to His Word, do it.

For added insights on this subject, it is recommended that you obtain Rick Renner's books *The Holy Spirit and You* and *Why We Need the Gifts of the Holy Spirit*. You may also select from Rick's other available resources by placing your order at **renner.org** or by calling 1-800-742-5593.

TOPIC

Two Works of Grace for Every Believer

SCRIPTURES

1. **Matthew 5:6** — Blessed are they which do hunger and thirst after righteousness: for they shall be filled.

2. **John 20:19-22** — Then the same day at evening, being the first day of the week, when the doors were shut where the disciples were assembled for fear of the Jews, came Jesus and stood in the midst, and saith unto them, Peace be unto you. And when he had so said, he shewed unto them his hands and his side. Then were the disciples glad, when they saw the Lord. Then said Jesus to them again, Peace be unto you: as my Father hath sent me, even so send I you. And when he had said this, he breathed on them, and saith unto them, Receive ye the Holy Ghost.

3. **Genesis 2:7** — And the Lord God formed man of the dust of the ground, and breathed into his nostrils the breath of life; and man became a living soul.

4. **Ephesians 1:13, 14** — In whom ye also trusted, after that ye heard the word of truth, the gospel of your salvation: in whom also after that ye believed, ye were sealed with that holy Spirit of promise, which is the earnest of our inheritance until the redemption of the purchased possession, unto the praise of his glory.

5. **1 Corinthians 6:19** — What? know ye not that your body is the temple of the Holy Ghost which is in you, which ye have of God, and ye are not your own?

6. **Luke 24:49** — And, behold, I send the promise of my Father upon you: but tarry ye in the city of Jerusalem, until ye be endued with power from on high.

GREEK WORDS

1. "breathed on them" — μ   (*emphusao*): to breathe into; to inflate
2. "receive" —   (*labete*): to take right now; to actively receive
3. "sealed" —   (*sphragidzo*): a seal placed on a package after the product had been examined and inspected to make sure it was fully intact and complete (the seal was proof that the product was flawless); the insignia of a wealthy person that guaranteed the package would be treated with tender care; a seal that guaranteed a package would make it to its final destination
4. "temple" —   (*naos*): a temple; a highly decorated shrine; the inner sanctum where a god lived
5. "behold" —   (*idou*): wow; look; see; a sense of amazement
6. "endued" —   (*enduo*): to be empowered; to clothe
7. "power" —   μ   (*dunamis*): explosive, superhuman power with enormous energy that produces phenomenal, extraordinary, and unparalleled results; the force of an entire army

SYNOPSIS

The five lessons in this study on *The Infilling of the Holy Spirit* will focus on the following topics:

1. Two Works of Grace for Every Believer
2. The New Testament Pattern for Being Filled With the Holy Spirit
3. Tongues — What Is It All About?
4. The Benefits of Being Filled With the Spirit
5. The Supernatural Role of the Holy Spirit in Your Life

The emphasis of this lesson:

To live the Christian life powerfully, it is vital to be filled with the Holy Spirit.

When the apostle Paul returned to the city of Ephesus, it is likely he took the inland road and entered the city through the Magnesia Gate. As he walked on the South Road, he met a group of disciples of John the Baptist. Notice how Paul initiated that conversation: "...Have ye received the Holy Ghost since ye believed?..." They responded, "...We have not so much as heard whether there be any Holy Ghost" (*see* Acts 19:2). These disciples had repented of their sins and had been baptized by John, expressing faith in the Messiah they believed would eventually come.

Paul informed them that the Messiah *indeed had come* and His name was Jesus Christ. Once they heard the Gospel message and believed on Christ, Paul water-baptized them and laid his hands on them in prayer to receive the baptism in the Holy Spirit. Acts 19:6 reveals, "…The Holy Ghost came on them; and they spake with tongues, and prophesied." Without question, Paul knew these new believers needed to be filled with the Holy Spirit immediately.

The same is true of believers today. To live the Christian life powerfully, it is vital to be filled with the Holy Spirit.

Salvation Is the Foundation — The *First* Work of Grace

There are two amazing works of God's grace offered to us, and the first is *salvation.*

Just after Jesus' resurrection from the dead, He appeared to the disciples who were hNIiding behind closed doors. After showing them His hands and side and convincing them it was really Him, Jesus said, "Peace be unto you: as my Father hath sent me, even so send I you. And when he had said this, he breathed on them, and saith unto them, Receive ye the Holy Ghost" (John 20:20, 21). It was in this moment that the disciples were born again under the New Covenant through Christ. This is the first time in human history that the new birth had occurred among mankind.

In the time of the Old Testament, the Spirit of God came upon people temporarily for a certain task. Once the task was completed, the Spirit of God would lift off the person and leave. The event recorded in John 20:21 is the first time the Spirit of God entered into people's lives *permanently.* This was a distinct, separate experience that preceded what happened to them on the day of Pentecost.

John 20:22 says Jesus "breathed on them." The word "breathed" is the Greek word *emphusao,* and it means *to breathe into* or *to inflate.* In that moment, Jesus Christ breathed His Spirit into their spirits. This is the same Greek word used in the Old Testament Septuagint in Genesis 2:7, where it says, "And the Lord God formed man of the dust of the ground, and *breathed into* his nostrils the breath of life; and man became a living soul." The phrase "breathed into" means God breathed into Adam in that very moment and inflated his lungs and brought him to life.

After Jesus breathed on the disciples, He said, "Receive ye the Holy Ghost" (John 20:22). The word "receive" is the Greek word *labete*, meaning *to take right now* or *to actively receive*. The use of *labete* signifies that Jesus was not prophesying and telling His disciples about what was going to happen later. On the contrary, He was urging them to receive His Spirit *in that very moment*. And that was the moment His disciples were born again.

When the Holy Spirit came into them and they were born again, peace flooded their lives. This is why Jesus said, "Peace be unto you," as they were born again. Peace is the primary fruit of salvation. Everyone who repents of their sin and calls on the name of the Lord to be saved receives the Holy Spirit and has peace with God. In fact, the moment you are saved, you are sealed with the Holy Spirit.

In that amazing moment when a person is born again, he or she becomes a new creature in Christ, receives the peace of God, and is sealed with the Holy Spirit.

The Scripture says, "…After that ye believed, ye were *sealed* with that Holy Spirit of promise" (Ephesians 1:13). The word "sealed" is the Greek word *sphragidzo*, and it describes *a seal placed on a package after it had been examined and inspected to make sure it was fully intact and complete* (the seal was proof that the product was flawless). The seal also guaranteed a package would make it to its final destination and be treated with utmost care.

Once the Holy Spirit enters our spirit and the blood of Jesus has cleansed us, we are born again and made flawless in God's eyes! His seal is placed on us, guaranteeing we have been fully checked out and found to be complete in Him.

The following is the *RIV* (*Renner's Interpretive Version*) of Ephesians 1:13 and 14:

When you were placed in Christ, God stamped you with a special seal and embossed it so deeply that it cannot be broken, erased, rubbed out, wiped out, deleted or removed; THAT unbreakable seal is the Holy Spirit. Once you were stamped

with Him, it meant you had God's approval. He examined the contents of your heart and found nothing flawed or inferior. And because everything was in order, He stamped you with the Holy Spirit, which is His seal of approval. Anyone who has this stamp is headed for special treatment. THIS seal means you belong to God and no one is to interfere with you as a "package."

This "Holy Spirit stamp" means the postage is prepaid to get you all the way to your ultimate destination. That means you can be sure that once your journey with the Lord begins, you are going to make it all the way to where God wants you to go! As good as all of this already seems, it's only the beginning of what God has planned for us.

You see, the Holy Spirit is the first installment of our full inheritance. In a certain sense, you could say the Holy Spirit is God's "down-payment" to show that He is serious and intends to complete the deal, finalize all the papers, put the product in His name, and finally make us His very own possession, with no one having the ability ever to exercise any claims or liens against us. When this whole process is finally wrapped up and the deal is completely done, we're all going to want to stand up and give God a glorious round of applause for everything He has done in our lives!

First Corinthians 6:19 says that once you are saved, "…your body is the temple of the Holy Ghost." The word "temple" is the Greek word *naos*, and in ancient cultures, it described *a highly decorated shrine or the inner sanctum where a god lived.* The moment you are saved, God's Spirit moves inside and takes up permanent residence! This is the first work of God's grace.

The Baptism in the Holy Spirit — The *Second* Work of Grace

After the disciples were born again and just before Jesus ascended into Heaven, He said to His disciples, "Behold, I send the promise of my Father upon you: but tarry ye in the city of Jerusalem, until ye be endued with power from on high" (Luke 24:49). Up until that point, the disciples had been saved and sealed with the Holy Spirit. If they had died at that moment, they would have gone to Heaven. They had become the "temple" of God, and His Spirit was living inside them. But there was more they needed, and Jesus told them to go to Jerusalem to wait for it.

The peace of God that the disciples received at the time of salvation was wonderful, but they needed more. They needed power. Jesus said, "Behold," which is the Greek word *idou*, and it means *wow; look; see*. This word carries with it *a sense of amazement*. In other words, Jesus was saying, "*Wow!* I am speechless concerning what you're about to receive!"

He then told them they would be "endued with power." The word "endued" is the Greek word *enduo*, meaning *to be empowered; to clothe*. The word "power" is the Greek word *dunamis*, and it indicates *explosive, superhuman power with enormous energy that produces phenomenal, extraordinary, and unparalleled results; the force of an entire army*. Within the context of this verse, Jesus told His disciples that as they waited in Jerusalem, *the explosive, superhuman power that produces extraordinary results would be placed inside them*.

Peace is the primary fruit of salvation, and *power* is the primary fruit of the baptism in the Holy Spirit.

This infilling of God's Spirit — the second work of grace for believers — is available to you! When you receive the baptism in the Holy Spirit, you will feel as if the full force of Heaven's army has come to live inside of you!

STUDY QUESTIONS

> **Study to shew thyself approved unto God, a workman that needeth not to be ashamed, rightly dividing the word of truth.**
> **— 2 Timothy 2:15**

1. In the time of the Old Testament, the Spirit of God came upon certain people for a certain task. Describe the reason the Spirit of God came upon Sampson (*see* Judges 15:11-20); Saul (*see* 1 Samuel 10:1-13); and David (*see* 1 Samuel 16:10-14). What was the result of this experience in their lives?

2. Peace is the primary fruit of salvation. The moment we repent of our sin and receive Jesus as our Lord and Savior, we have peace with God. Explain how this peace *with* God is different than the peace *of* God (*see* Philippians 4:6, 7; Colossians 3:15).

PRACTICAL APPLICATION

But be ye doers of the word, and not hearers only,
deceiving your own selves.
— James 1:22

1. Many believers have experienced the gift of salvation through faith in Jesus Christ — the first work of grace. It is likely that you are among them. But have you also received the baptism in the Holy Spirit — the *second* work of grace? If you *have* been filled with the Spirit, briefly share your experience and the changes that came into your life when you were first filled. If you have not been baptized in the Holy Spirit, do you know what may be hindering you?

2. According to Ephesians 1:13, when we repent of our sins and make Jesus the Lord and Savior of our life, we are "sealed with that Holy Spirit of promise." Carefully reread the Greek definition of the word "sealed" (*sphragidzo*). In what ways does this meaning encourage you? How would you share this eye-opening truth with a good friend who is struggling with condemnation?

LESSON 2

TOPIC

The New Testament Pattern for Being Filled With the Holy Spirit

SCRIPTURES

1. **John 20:21, 22** — Then said Jesus to them again, Peace be unto you: as my Father hath sent me, even so send I you. And when he had said this, he breathed on them, and saith unto them, Receive ye the Holy Ghost.

2. **Luke 24:49** — And, behold, I send the promise of my Father upon you: but tarry ye in the city of Jerusalem, until ye be endued with power from on high.

3. **Genesis 2:7** — And the Lord God formed man of the dust of the ground, and breathed into his nostrils the breath of life; and man became a living soul.

4. **Acts 1:4, 5** — And, being assembled together with them, commanded them that they should not depart from Jerusalem, but wait for the promise of the Father, which, saith he, ye have heard of me. For John truly baptized with water; but ye shall be baptized with the Holy Ghost not many days hence.

5. **Acts 2:1-4** — And when the day of Pentecost was fully come, they were all with one accord in one place. And suddenly there came a sound from heaven as a rushing mighty wind, and it filled all the house where they were sitting. And there appeared unto them cloven tongues like as of fire, and it sat upon each of them. And they were all filled with the Holy Ghost, and began to speak with other tongues, as the Spirit gave them utterance.

6. **Acts 8:12, 14, 15, 17-21** — When they believed Philip preaching the things concerning the kingdom of God, and the name of Jesus Christ, they were baptized, both men and women. Now when the apostles which were at Jerusalem heard that Samaria had received the word of God, they sent unto them Peter and John: who, when they were come down, prayed for them, that they might receive the Holy Ghost. Then laid they their hands on them, and they received the Holy Ghost. And when Simon saw that through laying on of the apostles' hands the Holy Ghost was given, he offered them money, saying, Give me also this power, that on whomsoever I lay hands, he may receive the Holy Ghost. But Peter said unto him, Thy money perish with thee, because thou hast thought that the gift of God may be purchased with money. Thou hast neither part nor lot in this matter: for thy heart is not right in the sight of God.

7. **1 Corinthians 14:18** — I thank my God, I speak with tongues more than ye all.

8. **Acts 9:17** — And Ananias went his way, and entered into the house; and putting his hands on him said, Brother Saul, the Lord, even Jesus, that appeared unto thee in the way as thou camest, hath sent me, that thou mightest receive thy sight, and be filled with the Holy Ghost.

9. **Acts 10:44, 46** — While Peter yet spake these words, the Holy Ghost fell on all them which heard the word. For they heard them speak with tongues, and magnify God....

10. **Acts 19:3-6** — And he said unto them, Unto what then were ye baptized? And they said, Unto John's baptism. Then, said Paul, John verily baptized with the baptism of repentance, saying unto the people, that they should believe on him which should come after him, that is, on Christ Jesus. When they heard this, they were baptized in the name of the Lord Jesus. And when Paul had laid his hands upon them, the Holy Ghost came on them; and they spake with tongues, and prophesied.

GREEK WORDS

1. "breathed on them" — μ (*emphusao*): to breathe into; to inflate

2. "power" — μ (*dunamis*): explosive, superhuman power with enormous energy that produces phenomenal, extraordinary, and unparalleled results; the force of an entire army

SYNOPSIS

The apostle Paul spent two years in Ephesus ministering at the School of Tyrannus, which was located in the heart of the city. Every morning and afternoon he taught a steady stream of people who came to the school seeking knowledge. Many signs and wonders took place during that time, including the salvation of many. These same people were also filled with the Holy Spirit.

God wants all believers everywhere to be filled with the explosive, superhuman power of His Spirit — *including you!* The infilling of the Holy Spirit is not a one-time event, but an ongoing experience in which we are filled again and again. The Holy Spirit's infilling unleashes a flood of divine power that enables us to operate mightily in His special spiritual gifts for the purpose of advancing God's Kingdom.

The emphasis of this lesson:

Although you don't have to be baptized in the Holy Spirit to be saved and go to Heaven, this second work of God's grace will infuse you with power to live life like you've never known or experienced.

In this lesson, the phrases "praying in tongues," "praying in the spirit," and "speaking in the spirit" are used interchangeably.

Jesus Initiated the Pattern

One of the last things Jesus instructed His disciples to do was to wait in the city of Jerusalem until they were "endued with power from on high" (*see* Luke 24:49). Luke records these words at the end of his Gospel. He then begins the book of Acts from this same moment in time. The Scripture says Jesus "being assembled together with them, commanded them that they should not depart from Jerusalem, but wait for the promise of the Father…" (Acts 1:4). This was not a suggestion; it was a *command*.

Jesus continued, "For John truly baptized with water; but ye shall be baptized with the Holy Ghost not many days hence" (Acts 1:5). This is the second work of grace Jesus was describing. Accordingly, the disciples waited in Jerusalem as they were instructed. They were already saved and on their way to Heaven, but they needed the power of the Holy Spirit to do the things Jesus did in His ministry on earth — and even *greater* works (*see* John 14:12).

It Began on the Day of Pentecost

Acts 2:1-4 tells us: "And when the day of Pentecost was fully come, they were all with one accord in one place. And suddenly there came a sound from heaven as a rushing mighty wind, and it filled all the house where they were sitting. And there appeared unto them cloven tongues like as of fire, and it sat upon each of them. And they were all filled with the Holy Ghost, and began to speak with other tongues, as the Spirit gave them utterance."

Here the pattern begins. We see that every time people were baptized in the Holy Spirit, they "began to speak with other tongues, as the Spirit gave them utterance." This pattern continues in Acts chapters 2, 8, 9, 10, and 19. Between Acts 2 and Acts 19, a period of 23 years had elapsed, and people were still being filled with the Spirit and speaking in other tongues.

It Happened in Samaria

In Acts chapter 8, which took place about one year after Pentecost, we see that Philip went to Samaria to preach the Gospel, and miracles took place. Demonic spirits were cast out of people, many who were lame began to walk, and those with palsies (paralysis) were healed. "When they believed Philip preaching the things concerning the kingdom of God, and the name of Jesus Christ, they were baptized, both men and women" (Acts 8:12).

People heard the Gospel and saw firsthand the power of God manifested. They repented of their sins and received Christ into their lives. They were saved and subsequently baptized in water as a confirmation. They were born again and on their way to Heaven. They had *peace* with God, but they also needed His *power*.

Acts 8:14 and 15 reveals, "Now when the apostles which were at Jerusalem heard that Samaria had received the word of God, they sent unto them Peter and John: who, when they were come down, prayed for them, that they might receive the Holy Ghost." Salvation, the first work of grace, had been experienced by the Samaritans. The second work of grace had not been experienced — *until* Peter and John "laid they their hands on them, and they received the Holy Ghost" (Acts 8:17). This is a reference to this second work of grace that is called the baptism in the Holy Spirit.

When the apostles laid their hands on the people, something supernatural happened. It was so visible and tangible that a professed sorcerer named Simon offered Peter and John money to empower him to do the same. Peter rejected Simon's offer, declaring, "Thou hast neither part nor lot in this matter: for thy heart is not right in the sight of God" (v. 21). The word "matter" confirms the Samaritans spoke in tongues. It is the Greek word *logos*, meaning *words* or *speaking*. Peter literally told Simon, "You have neither part nor lot *in this kind of speaking.*"

It Happened in the Life of Saul (Paul)

In Acts 9, we see Saul traveling on the road to Damascus, bent on imprisoning followers of Christ. Suddenly, he was knocked to the ground by a brilliant light from Heaven. The voice of Jesus spoke to him saying, "...Saul, Saul, why persecutes me?. . ." Saul responded, "...Who art thou, Lord?. . ." Jesus said, "...I am Jesus whom thou persecutest..." (Acts 9:4, 5).

Notice Saul called Jesus *Lord*. No one can do this unless they are saved (*see* 1 Corinthians 12:3). In that moment on the Damascus road, Saul was born again, and the Spirit of God took up permanent residence inside him. He had peace with God and was on his way to Heaven. Yet there was more Saul needed. He needed *power*. That's what God sent him through the hands of Ananias: "And Ananias went his way, and entered into the house; and putting his hands on him said, Brother Saul, the Lord, even Jesus, that appeared unto thee in the way as thou camest, hath sent me, that thou mightest receive thy sight, and be filled with the Holy Ghost" (Acts 9:17).

Although Acts 9 doesn't specifically say Saul (Paul) spoke in tongues, we know that he did. In First Corinthians 14:18, he said, "I thank my God, I speak with tongues more than ye all."

Paul's salvation and baptism in the Holy Spirit took place about *four years* after Pentecost!

It Happened in the Life of Cornelius and His Household

In Acts 10, about *seven years* after Pentecost, we find Peter visiting the home of a godly Gentile named Cornelius. Peter began to share the Gospel message, and Scripture says that while he "yet spake these words, the Holy Ghost fell on all them which heard the word" (Acts 10:44). Verse 46 confirms, "For they heard them speak with tongues, and magnify God...."

This was a remarkable occurrence that had never before happened. In one moment, Gentiles were both saved and baptized in the Holy Spirit. Both works of God's grace happened simultaneously. Again, the pattern is seen: People were *saved, filled with the Holy Spirit*, and *spoke with other tongues*.

It Happened in Ephesus — 23 Years After Pentecost!

By the time we get to Acts 19, approximately *23 years* had passed since the day of Pentecost. The apostle Paul had made his way to Ephesus and encountered a group of men who had heard the preaching of John the Baptist and had received his baptism of repentance. They were not born again; they were waiting for the arrival of the Messiah that John prophesied would come.

Paul informed them the Messiah had indeed come, and His name was Jesus Christ (*see* Acts 19:4). They were then born again, sealed with the Spirit of God, and on their way to Heaven. They had *peace* with God, but they needed the *power* of God.

Paul knew they needed the second work of grace to live powerfully for Jesus. Therefore, "...When Paul had laid his hands upon them, the Holy Ghost came on them; and they spake with tongues, and prophesied" (Acts 19:6).

The pattern of receiving Christ (salvation), followed by baptism in the Holy Spirit and speaking in tongues, was God's way of working in the Church throughout the entire book of Acts.

It is still Christ's pattern of working in our lives today.

STUDY QUESTIONS

Study to shew thyself approved unto God, a workman that needeth not to be ashamed,rightly dividing the word of truth.
— 2 Timothy 2:15

1. The Holy Spirit was promised by Jesus to be given to His disciples and followers at the time they became born again. This initiated a pattern in Acts 2 that can also be seen in chapters 8, 9, 10, and 19. Briefly describe this pattern.

2. Since receiving salvation and the baptism in the Holy Spirit was the pattern in the book of Acts — and it is still God's pattern today — what can you conclude about God's will for *your* life? Since this is God's pattern, doesn't it communicate that this is the pattern He wants to work in your life too? If you have not received the baptism in the Holy Spirit, what is stopping you from receiving it today?

PRACTICAL APPLICATION

But be ye doers of the word, and not hearers only, deceiving your own selves.
— James 1:22

1. The primary fruit of the baptism in the Holy Spirit is power (*dunamis*). It is defined as "explosive, superhuman power with enormous energy that produces phenomenal, extraordinary, and unparalleled results." In your own words, share why you need the Spirit's power in your daily life. In what specific ways are you presently drawing on His power? In what areas do you sense you need to begin drawing more on this explosive, superhuman power?

2. The moment you were saved, the Holy Spirit came into your spirit, and you were instantly born again. That's when the Spirit sealed you and took up permanent residence within you. Briefly share how the

salvation experience is different from the baptism in the Holy Spirit as it is seen in the book of Acts.

TOPIC

Tongues — What Is It All About?

SCRIPTURES

1. **Matthew 12:34** — O generation of vipers, how can ye being evil, speak good things? for out of the abundance of the heart the mouth speaketh.

2. **John 4:24** — God is a Spirit: and they that worship him must worship him in spirit and in truth.

3. **1 Corinthians 14:2, 4** — For he that speaketh in an unknown tongue speaketh not unto men, but unto God: for no man understandeth him; howbeit in the spirit he speaketh mysteries. He that speaketh in an unknown tongue edifieth himself; but he that prophesieth edifieth the church.

4. **1 Corinthians 14:18** — I thank my God, I speak with tongues more than ye all.

GREEK WORDS

1. "edifieth" — μ (*oikodome*): an architectural term meaning to enlarge or amplify a house; it depicts the careful following of an architectural plan to enlarge, increase, or amplify; to edify; to improve; to leave in an improved condition

SYNOPSIS

In the heart of Ephesus, at a place called the Philosopher's Square, the apostle Paul and Aquila and Priscilla spent a lot of time ministering the Gospel to those who were hungry to know more about Christ. It was also a place where Paul taught on the ministry of the Holy Spirit.

Again and again, nonbelievers witnessed the manifestation of the power of God. Undoubtedly, they had questions. Hence, they gathered at Philosopher's Square to hear Paul teach. It was to the Church of Ephesus that Paul wrote many amazing truths about the Holy Spirit — about being sealed with the Spirit, being filled with the Spirit, and the power of praying in the spirit.

Since the early believers in Ephesus needed the infilling of the Holy Spirit, we certainly need that same experience today.

In this lesson, the phrases "praying in tongues," "praying in the spirit," and "speaking in the spirit" are used interchangeably.

The emphasis of this lesson:

Out of the abundance of your heart, your mouth will speak. It is a principle that cannot be denied. The mouth is the outlet of the human spirit.

Your Mouth Is the Outlet of Your Spirit

In Mathew 12:34, Jesus said, "…Out of the abundance of the heart the mouth speaketh." Whatever your heart is full of is going to come out of your mouth. All you need to do to discover what is inside you is listen to the words that are coming out of your mouth.

If you're filled with fear, you will speak fearful words. If you're filled with anger, you will speak angry words. If you're filled with bitterness, bitter words will make their way through your lips.

What happens if your heart is filled with the Holy Spirit? The words that come from your mouth will be full of the *Spirit*. Throughout the book of Acts, when people were filled with the Holy Spirit, out of the abundance of what was in their hearts, they spoke. Specifically, they spoke in tongues, which is the language of the Spirit. The Samaritans, the apostle Paul, Cornelius and his household, the disciples of John in Ephesus, and countless others were all filled with the Spirit and spoke the language of the Spirit.

The Real You Is a Spirit

In John 4:24, Jesus said, "God is a Spirit: and they that worship him must worship him in spirit and in truth." You are created in the image of God (*see* Genesis 1:27). You are a spirit that has a soul and lives in a body (*see*

1 Thessalonians 5:23). What you see in the mirror is not the real you; the real you is your spirit that will live forever.

God is a Spirit and you are a spirit. What language does a spirit speak? *Spirit speaks spirit.* Just as a Russian speaks Russian, a German speaks German, and a Spaniard speaks Spanish, a spirit speaks spirit. Your spirit desires to speak to God in a spiritual language, not a natural language.

When we pray in tongues, we pray in the language of the spirit; our spirit is speaking directly to God. The spiritual language of tongues supersedes any human language. It is not just gibberish or noise. It is the language of the human spirit. But we can only speak this language of the Spirit when we are filled with the Holy Spirit — He gives us the "utterance" to do so. The Holy Spirit miraculously looses the "tongue" of our human spirit and we are able to speak directly to God without hindrance — spirit to Spirit.

Why Speak the Language of the Spirit?

One of the biggest reasons Satan stirs up fear and creates confusion over this topic is so we won't communicate directly to God in a spiritual language. Although praying in our native language builds our mind and can help us discern the will of God, that language is limited. On the other hand, praying in the spirit in other tongues is *limitless.* Our spirit can express things that our mind can never express in our natural language. Therefore, when we shift from praying in our natural language to praying in our heavenly language, we shift into the highest, most supernatural level of prayer available.

In First Corinthians 14, we discover some of the important reasons why we speak in tongues. Verse 2 says, "He that speaketh in an unknown tongue speaketh not unto men, but unto God: for no man understandeth him; howbeit in the spirit he speaketh mysteries." This indicates that when you speak in tongues — a spiritual language "unknown" to you in the natural — you bypass your mind and speak directly to God. It is spirit-to-Spirit communication.

This verse also says that when you speak in the language of the spirit, you speak "mysteries." The moment you were saved, God's plan for your life was deposited into your spirit by His Spirit. Your mind doesn't know this divine plan. However, there is a way to move God's plan from your spirit to your mind, and it is by praying in the spirit's language. When you speak in tongues, you literally release the hidden secrets of God; you draw His will up out of your spirit and into your mind where you gain understanding.

Paul went on to say in First Corinthians 14:4, "He that speaketh in an unknown tongue edifieth himself. ..." The word "edify" is a Greek architectural term that was used to describe increasing the size of an existing building. When a building was not big enough, a builder would break out its walls to expand the square footage. Paul uses this word "edifieth" to indicate that when we pray in tongues, we expand our spiritual walls, increasing our spiritual capacity.

Realize that Paul, whom God used to write these verses, said, "I thank my God, I speak with tongues more than ye all" (1 Corinthians 14:18). By speaking in tongues, Paul edified himself greatly. He greatly expanded his spiritual capacity and was able to take in so much revelation that he wrote nearly two thirds of the New Testament.

Humbly Exercise Your Privilege

If you speak in tongues, you should never make those who don't speak in tongues feel inferior or like a second-class Christian. Nevertheless, if you don't speak in tongues, you are missing something amazing that God has made available for you. You might ask, "Do I have to speak in tongues to go to Heaven?" *No.*

"Do I have to speak in tongues to have a relationship with God?" Again, the answer is no.

The truth is, you don't *have* to speak in tongues — you *get* to speak in tongues. It is a privilege of spirit-to-Spirit communication, the highest level of interaction with God that is available! If you want a greater spiritual capacity, begin speaking the language of the spirit with greater regularity. If you have not been baptized in the Holy Spirit but would like to be, begin to seek God and ask Him to pour out His Spirit into your life (*see* Luke 11:9-13; Acts 2:38, 39).

STUDY QUESTIONS

Study to shew thyself approved unto God, a workman that needeth not to be ashamed, rightly dividing the word of truth.
— 2 Timothy 2:15

1. In Matthew 12:34, Jesus said, "Out of the abundance of the heart the mouth speaketh." Stop and think about the words and phrases that

come out of your mouth on a regular basis. Do you see a pattern? What recurring words or phrases freely flow from your lips? What does this reveal about what's in your heart?

2. Praying in tongues is not gibberish or just noise. It is the language of the human spirit empowered by the Holy Spirit. According to First Corinthians 14:4 and Jude 1:20, what can you expect to happen when you pray in tongues? How do these truths motivate you to pray?

3. First Corinthians 14:2 states, "He that speaketh in an unknown tongue speaketh not unto men, but unto God: for no man understandeth him; howbeit in the spirit he speaketh mysteries." What does this verse say to you?

PRACTICAL APPLICATION

But be ye doers of the word, and not hearers only,
deceiving your own selves.
— James 1:22

1. You are a spirit being who has a soul and lives in a body. In both First Corinthians 6:19 and Second Corinthians 6:16, it says that the body is "the temple of the Holy Spirit" — it's the physical house in which He lives and works. Be honest. How would you describe the way you are taking care of the Holy Spirit's house? Is there an area of your body you have neglected that is affecting your soul and spirit? If so, where? What steps do you feel the Holy Spirit is prompting you to take to get His house — your body — in order?

2. Very likely you have heard someone say, "Do I *have to* speak in tongues?" What might cause a person to shy away from wanting the privilege of being able to communicate spirit-to-Spirit with the Creator of the universe? After studying this lesson, what words of wisdom and encouragement could you now offer someone else?

TOPIC

The Benefits of Being Filled With the Spirit

SCRIPTURES

1. **Ephesians 5:15-21** — See then that ye walk circumspectly, not as fools, but as wise, Redeeming the time, because the days are evil. Wherefore be ye not unwise, but understanding what the will of the Lord is. And be not drunk with wine, wherein is excess; but be filled with the Spirit. Speaking to yourselves in psalms and hymns and spiritual songs, singing and making melody in your heart to the Lord; giving thanks always for all things unto God and the Father in the name of our Lord Jesus Christ; submitting yourselves one to another in the fear of God.

2. **Matthew 12:34** — O generation of vipers, how can ye being evil, speak good things? for out of the abundance of the heart the mouth speaketh.

GREEK WORDS

1. "walk" — ϖ ϖ (*peripateo*): to walk around; to habitually walk; one's lifestyle

2. "circumspectly" — (*akribos*): accurately; carefully; exactly; circumspectly

3. "fools" — (*asophos*): unenlightened; unintelligent; foolish

4. "wise" — (*sophos*): enlightened; intelligent; cultivated

5. "redeeming" — (*exagoradzo*): to buy back; to redeem; to make the most of

6. "unwise" — (*aphron*): unintelligent; brainless

7. "understanding" — μ (*suniemi*): a coming together; putting all the pieces together; understanding

8. "drunk" — μ (*methusko*): to excessively drink alcohol; a drunkard

9. "filled" — ϖ   (*pleroo*): to fill to capacity; to fill to the full

10. "psalms" — μ (*psalmos*): songs of praise

11. "hymns" — μ (*humnos*): sacred compositions, the primary goal of which is to give glory and honor to God

12. "spiritual songs" —   ϖ μ   (*odais pneumatikais*): songs in the spirit; singing in the spirit; singing in tongues

13. "melody" —   (*psallo*): to pluck the strings of a harp or bow; a heartfelt expression of music

14. "giving thanks" —   (*eucharisteo*): an overwhelmingly good feeling about someone or something; a free-flowing thankfulness; gratitude

15. "submitting" — ϖ   (*hupotasso*): obedience to authority; submission to authority in any context; one who is under authority; to defer to someone else

SYNOPSIS

Being filled with the Holy Spirit is an amazing experience! The Spirit influences everything in our lives — the way we see, hear, think, and act. This is so important that the apostle Paul urged the church of Ephesus to be filled with the Spirit continually. History shows that they *started* in the power of God, and they *continued* in the power of God for many years.

However, when Paul wrote to the church of Ephesus, they were experiencing some major problems. They were dealing with gossip and backbiting that was producing malice and bitterness in hearts of many. Although they had been walking with the Lord for a long time, they were not acting very mature at the time of Paul's writing. Paul identified their ungodly attitudes and behavior in Ephesians chapter 4.

Emphasis of this lesson:

When you are filled with the Holy Spirit and come under His influence, you are changed! Your thinking, feelings, perspective, and the atmosphere of your life become more positive and life-giving. A spiritual dimension opens for you that is unequaled.

As in previous lessons, in this segment, the phrases "praying in tongues," "praying in the spirit," and "speaking in the spirit" are used interchangeably.

Live Life on a Higher Level

In Ephesians 5:15, Paul said, "See then that ye walk circumspectly, not as fools, but as wise." The word "walk" is from the Greek term *peripateo*, meaning *to walk around, to habitually walk*, and it also referred to *one's lifestyle*. Essentially, Paul was calling the Ephesians to move up higher and stop treating each other so badly. He was urging them to begin living a new lifestyle.

How were they to walk? Paul said "circumspectly" — the Greek word *akribos*, which means *accurately, carefully*, or *exactly*. Then he said, "…Not as fools, but as wise." The word "fools" is from the Greek word *asophos*, and it simply indicates *unenlightened* or *unintelligent*. The word wise is *sophos*, meaning *intelligent, cultured*, or *enlightened*. Paul was saying, "Quit all this foolish behavior and stop acting unintelligent. Begin acting like the intelligent, cultured believers I know you can be."

Paul continued in verse 16 saying, "Redeeming the time, because the days are evil." "Redeeming" is the Greek word *exagoradzo* — a combination of the word *ex*, meaning *out*, and *agoradzo*, meaning *I buy*. The word *exagoradzo* literally means *to buy back, to redeem*, or *to make the most of*. Basically, Paul was saying, "Buy back the time you've lost and make the most of each opportunity you still have." The Ephesians had lost or forsaken opportunities to enjoy and appreciate each other because of their poor behavior.

See the Big Picture!

In verse 17, Paul went on to say, "Wherefore be ye not unwise, but understanding what the will of the Lord is." Here, the word "unwise" is the Greek word *aphron*, meaning *unintelligent* or *brainless*. The word "understanding" is the Greek word *suniemi*, and it describes *a coming together, putting all the pieces together*. It is like putting together the many pieces of a jigsaw puzzle to reveal the big picture. Paul was saying, "Don't be brainless; bring all the pieces together to see and understand the big picture of what God wants to do in life."

What was the "big picture" of the will of God that He wanted the Ephesians — *and us* — to understand? Paul gives the answer in verse 18: "And be not drunk with wine, wherein is excess; but be filled with the Spirit." The word "drunk" is the Greek word *methusko*, which means *to excessively drink alcohol, a drunkard*. Paul's use of the Greek here emphatically communicated to the Ephesians, "Stop it and stop it now! I want you to stop being habitually drunk."

Instead, Paul said, "…Be filled with the Spirit." The word "filled" is the Greek word *pleroo*, which means *to fill to capacity*, *to fill to the full*. It's important to note that the tense of this verb indicates perpetual activity. "Be filled" actually means *be BEING filled*. Although the initial baptism in the Holy Spirit is an incredible event in our lives, we are not supposed to stop there. We are to be *continually* filled with the Spirit.

In a previous lesson, we learned that as we pray in the language of the spirit, we "edify" ourselves. That is, we expand our spiritual capacity for more of God in our lives. Unfortunately, many believers live just "touched" by the Spirit. But God wants us to be *filled to full capacity* with His Spirit — *continually*. This is the will of the Lord for you and me.

Being Filled With the Spirit Is Life-Transforming

Paul described some of the effects of being filled with the Spirit in Ephesians 5:19-21. He said, "Speaking to yourselves in psalms and hymns and spiritual songs, singing and making melody in your heart to the Lord; giving thanks always for all things unto God and the Father in the name of our Lord Jesus Christ; submitting yourselves one to another in the fear of God." These verses reveal a changed person. He or she is controlled by the Spirit of God.

The word "psalms" is the Greek word *psalmos*, which simply means *a song of praise*. The word "hymns" is the Greek word *humnos*, which describes *a sacred composition designed to give glory to God*. "Spiritual songs" is the Greek phrase *odais pneumatikais*, and it signifies *songs in the spirit, singing in the spirit*, or *singing in tongues*. All these words confirm that when you are filled with the Spirit, the overflow of what is in your heart will come out of your mouth.

Also in verse 19 is the phrase, "…making melody in your heart to the Lord." The word "melody" is the Greek word *psallo*, which means *to pluck the strings of a harp or bow*; *a heartfelt expression of music*. In this passage, the instrument is not a harp or bow; it is the heart itself singing to the Lord.

In verse 20, Paul revealed that one filled with the Spirit will be "giving thanks always." "Giving thanks" is taken from the Greek word *eucharisteo*, and it signifies *an overwhelmingly good feeling about someone or something, a free-flowing thankfulness and gratitude.* Instead of being ungrateful and focusing on what we *don't* have, we are very thankful and focused on what we *do* have.

In verse 21, we see that "submitting yourselves one to another in the fear of God" is also a result of being filled with the Spirit. The word "submitting" is the Greek word *hupotasso,* and it means *obedience to authority, submission to authority in any context, one who is under authority, to defer to someone else.* When we are filled with and controlled by the Holy Spirit, it makes it easier for us to submit to authority and defer to others.

These life-producing characteristics reflect just some of the many benefits of being filled with the Spirit.

STUDY QUESTIONS

Study to shew thyself approved unto God, a workman that needeth
not to be ashamed, rightly dividing the word of truth.
— 2 Timothy 2:15

1. In Ephesians 5:18, we are told not to be drunk with wine but to be filled with the Holy Spirit instead. Describe some of the common effects that intoxication causes on one's mood, thinking, and behavior. How might being filled with the Spirit affect the way you think, speak, and act in a *positive* way?

2. The believers in the Church of Ephesus had been behaving very badly. According to Ephesians 4:25-32, what kind of things had they been doing? Be honest: Are you exhibiting any of these behaviors? If so, which ones? What do you need to do to make things right with God and those you may have hurt?

3. How would those closest to you describe your life — as Spirit-*touched* or Spirit-*filled?* What evidence might they offer to back up their claim?

But be ye doers of the word, and not hearers only,
deceiving your own selves.
—James 1:22

1. It appears that the believers in the Church of Ephesus were frequently reaching for wine and becoming totally intoxicated — possibly to cope with the stress and challenges of life. Stop and think about it. What are the top three stressors in *your* life? When the pressure is on, how do you deal with that pressure?

2. Are you reaching for something other than the Word or the Spirit of God to cope with life or dull pain? If so, what is it? How do the truths found in Ephesians 5:15-21 encourage you to begin living your life filled with the Spirit?

LESSON 5

TOPIC

The Supernatural Role of the Holy Spirit in Your Life

SCRIPTURES

1. **Ephesians 5:18** — And be not drunk with wine, wherein is excess; but be filled with the Spirit.

2. **Romans 8:26** — Likewise the Spirit also helpeth our infirmities: for we know not what we should pray for as we ought: but the Spirit itself maketh intercession for us with groanings which cannot be uttered.

GREEK WORDS

1. "what" — (*ti*): minute, minuscule detail, exactly, explicitly

2. "ought" — (*dei*): an obligation or necessity

3. "intercession" — ω (*huperentugchano*): to fall into a ditch with someone else; the process of rescuing someone from a ditch; pictures one who comes upon someone who has fallen into

some kind of quandary; upon discovering the trapped person's dilemma, he joins the victim and implements a rescue and deliverance for the one in trouble; conveys the idea of a rescue operation; to appeal to God on behalf of someone; an action that results in one being delivered from imminent danger.

SYNOPSIS

The church of Ephesus was started through the ministry of Paul in the First Century. During that time, a revival of magnificent proportions broke out in the city and eventually affected the entire province of Asia. Thousands upon thousands of people were saved, many of the sick were radically healed, and people were set free from demonic bondage. What took place was truly supernatural.

In Ephesians 5:18, Paul said to believers, both then and now, "Be not drunk with wine, wherein is excess; but be filled with the Spirit." As we learned in the last lesson, the Greek language indicates being *continually* filled to the full with the Holy Spirit. Regardless of how much of the Spirit you had previously, God wants you to have more and more of the Spirit with each passing day. He wants you to be *being filled* continually. When you are filled with the Holy Spirit, you are positioned for the supernatural to take place.

The emphasis of this lesson:

Praying in tongues releases the power of God in ways that nothing else can. It is a supernatural level of prayer that brings you into a deeper dimension than you could ever get into by yourself. Instead of just blindly dealing with symptoms, the Holy Spirit prays with you and through you, cutting to the core to reveal and deal with root issues. This is God's promise to you and every believer who is filled with the Spirit.

In Romans 8:26, the apostle Paul said, "Likewise the Spirit also helpeth our infirmities: for we know not what we should pray for as we ought: but the Spirit itself maketh intercession for us with groanings which cannot be uttered." Here we discover our primary problem in life — ignorance. We often don't know what to do, what to say, or what to pray in the situations in which we find ourselves.

The Holy Spirit Makes Accurate Intercession for Us

In the phrase, "…For we know not what we should pray for as we ought…," the word "what" is the Greek term *ti*, which describes *the most minute, minuscule detail*. The word "ought" is the Greek word *dei*, and it describes *an obligation or necessity*. Essentially, this is saying, we don't know how to specifically pray in the way each new situation necessitates. We can't pray about our new challenges in the same way we prayed for previous ones. There are different facets involved, so it requires a different type of prayer. This will be true of each new challenge we face.

There is no human being who excels in prayer enough to know how to accurately pray in each situation. Regardless of how much of the Word we know, we need the supernatural working of the Holy Spirit in our lives. He is the only One who can illuminate what is going on and accurately direct us on how to pray and what to do.

The Holy Spirit Releases His Power Toward Us Through Prayer

Paul continued by saying, "…The Spirit itself [Himself] maketh intercession for us with groanings which cannot be uttered." The word "intercession" is *huperentugchano* in the Greek, which means *to fall into a ditch with someone else and begin the process of rescuing that individual from the ditch*. Not knowing what to pray in the challenging situations we face is like being in a ditch of ignorance. Yet the moment we cry out for the Holy Spirit's help, He falls in right beside us, meeting us in our place of struggle and rescuing us from our trouble.

The Spirit does this with "groanings which cannot be uttered." This primarily refers to praying in tongues, the language of the Spirit. This is such a privileged and powerful form of prayer because the Holy Spirit can see what you can't see, and He knows what you don't know. As you learn to partner with Him and get involved where He needs you, you will see incredible, supernatural things take place!

STUDY QUESTIONS

Study to shew thyself approved unto God, a workman that needeth
not to be ashamed,rightly dividing the word of truth.
— 2 Timothy 2:15

1. For believers in the Early Church, receiving the baptism in the Holy
   Spirit was viewed as mandatory if they were going to walk in the
   power of God. Why do you think this was the case? How do you see
   the baptism in the Holy Spirit — as optional or mandatory? Explain
   your answer.

2. Understanding the purpose, power, and outcomes of praying in the
   spirit is priceless. Take a few minutes to read and meditate on these
   two passages: Romans 8:26 and 27 and First Corinthians 2:9-13.
   What is the Holy Spirit revealing to you in these verses about His
   work in and through your life?

PRACTICAL APPLICATION

But be ye doers of the word, and not hearers only,
deceiving your own selves.
— James 1:22

1. Knowing how to accurately pray in any given situation is impossible
   to do on our own. However, through the supernatural power of the
   Holy Spirit, He "…maketh intercession for us with groanings which
   cannot be uttered" (Romans 8:26). Can you remember a challenging
   situation in which you were clueless on how to pray, but after you
   began praying in the Spirit, you were illuminated about what to pray
   and do? Briefly describe what happened and share how it encourages
   you to pray in the spirit more.

2. Are you or someone you love currently in a challenging situation in
   which you are clueless as how to pray or what to do — a situation that
   has left you feeling hopeless and overwhelmed? If so, describe it. Why
   not take time right now to pray and allow the Holy Spirit to "fall in
   the ditch with you"? By faith, pray in tongues and allow the Spirit to
   make "intercession" for you "with groanings which cannot be uttered."
   After praying, write down how the Holy Spirit directs you and the
   outcome of your obedience.

www.ingramcontent.com/pod-product-compliance
Lightning Source LLC
Chambersburg PA
CBHW060559030426
42337CB00019B/3571